Twilight of Dreams

Tom McFadden

Plain View Press
P. O. 42255
Austin, TX 78704

plainviewpress.net
sb@plainviewpress.net
1-512-441-2452

Copyright Tom McFadden, 2007. All rights reserved.
ISBN: 978-1-891386-33-6
Library of Congress Number: 2007942845

Cover art by Nancy Holthus: "Dream Woods"

Contents

The Other Side	5
Almost Falling	6
Alone in the Crowd	7
Evening Ice Cream	9
Face in a Heather Field	10
Knocking at a Hollow Door	11
Such a Rain	12
The Portrait	13
The Maybe Sky	15
Gaspings	16
Appropriate Attire	17
Chablis and the River Lee	18
Echoes of Yesteryear	20
Ghost in the Parking Lot	21
The Prelude Pause	22
Flying	24
A Burning Desire	26
Gliding	27
Holding Starlight	28
The Follow Place	29
A Ladder Not Long Enough	31
The Other Side of the Window	32
Partner in the Dark	33
Too Far Away	34
Made in Heaven	35
The Empty Chair	36
The Night Unwritten	37
A Little Flower Song	38
Cry from a Separate Solitude	40
The Silver Derby	42
Going Nowhere	43
Blendings	44
Last Friend	46
In Mid-Air	47
Leaf Rain	49
Final Applause	50
The Dream Pendant	52
Tilted Sadness	54
Night Talk	55

Slipped from the Window	57
The Thinning Dark	59
Last Ride into Midnight	61
Wall of Time	62
The Lost Thing	63
Retracings	65
In Someone Else's Time	66
The Nothing Pond	67
Broken Parallel	69
The Color of Time	70
Rain from Another Sky	71
Falling out of Day	72
Last Posture	73
The Way Lost	74
Pouring Night	75
Epilogue Clouds	76
Discountenance	77
The Dark at the Door	78
The Walking Stick	79
The Return Trip	80
The Glass Dwelling	81
Where Once Was Day	82
Twilight of Dreams	83

The Other Side

The end of the road narrows
into final, yet disparate, strides:
a last burst of dreams…
then, the lost travel to the other side.

Dreams shine here,
in this life-clinging half
—this complex's independent side—
glow-drifting through halls
however they can
to extinguishment defy.
Some dreams pass at a tilt, leaning on canes,
while others roll with walker wheels,
and others, still, assume motorized scooters
to fly fast above the rug, dreamed high,
like comets of the corridors:
each burning and ending,
yet resplendent in its hopefully long goodbye.

Cognizance twists toward the other side,
like fearful eyes in moment's shift
against the dreaded beckoning.
Linger in memory those previous dreamers
whose eyes fell dull
and who finally lost their way through the halls—
with lost travel realized to the healthcare side
to join that hollow prelude
to the dark beyond the door.

Although the extant dreamers know
that the road for them must also narrow,
it is here they cling to stay:
from that fall toward the dark at the other side,
one last-light's step away.

Almost Falling

The walker wheels seemed sufficiently aligned
with the sides of the stuffed chair behind her,
so that, after multiple, quick, anxiety-laden, extra looks
from the corner of one eye,
with a small gasp at the edge of life's cliff,
she let go—into backward and downward tilt.
Stress quickened across the face during uncertain flight,
then subsided as the time-widened behind
once more landed safely, wedging into the chair.
Eyes closed to join a long exhale, then reopened.
It had come to this, this metamorphosis:
certainty's surrender into the conditional.
Now, sitting was almost falling.

But, grateful she had not missed the chair,
she adjusted her landed posture—
ready, once more, to daydream backward.
This time it was her mind that tilted back and down.
Heck, once she had almost been a movie star—
well, an extra…in three or four films.
If one of the other agents had looked at her
at just the right angle
at just the right time—
who knows?
Maybe if one head had just turned…
Maybe she had been almost there, one chance away from the top!
And once she *had* been goosed by a star!
She laughed out loud at the memory.
Let's see. What exactly had he looked like?
She could almost remember.
And how had *she* looked, exactly, then?
Maybe…if she would just tilt a little more—
a little more back and a little more down—
she could almost remember how she had almost been.

Alone in the Crowd

A shy face, worry-tight,
slowly rounded the entrance frame,
eyes quickly up and down
to see, yet not see, that elegant space,
as if from a hiding place.
Oh, my! It was so crowded!
But, why not?
This was an expensive retirement place,
and the food possessed such taste…
as did they, the formers of the crowd—
so relaxed and appropriate,
so shaped to fit in,
knowing where every utensil should fall,
and so easily sociable, all.

She would choose this chair by the wall,
and try to remain innocuous,
where she would just quietly sit,
in case they might fear her one of the parts
that really did not quite fit.
She could *feel* their pulsation,
but not join such rhythm,
able just to descend more tightly into herself
until she felt almost dizzy and strange.
And wasn't it unusual
how dark the day itself had framed,
there in the dinner windows,
as though from an uncharted eclipse's fall?

There, in the beautiful gathering place,
long after hours,
long after all the day's meals
had been served,
conversations voiced,
tables cleaned,

continued

exits made,
and even echoes
floated away…
there had she entered dimness
to populate the vacancy.
Within missing light,
the lone figure, too, now seemed
hard to discern,
that vast room's slightest sight, barely there,
surrounded by empty tables and chairs;
nor could she be well heard,
for she had chosen a profile
unevoking and still,
striving not to disturb
a roomful of diners not really there—
polite and assuring to not be too loud
while she sat there, alone in the crowd.

Evening Ice Cream

A door which needed a code
had risen between them,
Bill left to travel each day
from their apartment for two
on the retirement side,
through the double security doors,
to the healthcare side of the complex
for their sharing of evening ice cream.

In her new room,
he would always pull a chair
as close to the bed as he could
for their traditional treat of that frozen form,
while it should hold its solidity.
And while he would utter her name,
but she not his,
the spoon would rise, and rise again,
toward a blank face
that he would call "dear."

The corners of her mouth
would he gently scoop and re-scoop
with brushes of spoon-edge.
Yet, at times, a catch of remembrance
would pull him into reveries;
and, while he sat frozen, drifted away,
the white near her mouth would slowly melt
until a large, evening drop
would flow on its way,
down that great blankness,
unable to stay.

Face in a Heather Field

Once it was a Holocaust face,
with stares of Nazis upon it like erosion,
to wear the features away;
yet, even now, though assaulted and aging,
the contours of her visage
linger in their survival.

Evocatively worrisome,
the expression of that face
now wanders, more and more,
and I hope she not be
traveling back, through mental scars,
to redream a nightmare lived.
I fear her doors may reburst open
and into the middle of the street
she be recalled.
Too cruel it would seem
to be marched away twice.

I wish her no presence back into that night,
but in this stay of light,
where the echo of boot heels
may yield to the innocuous step
of security guard footwear,
compassionately walking these nursing home halls,
for, disparate and distant
from nightmare twice fallen,
it is I, now, who is her guard—
a son of the shamrock.

From swastika to shamrock,
I will try to keep the train away,
with no one-way trip on the railroad line.
I will keep her in a heather field,
where stares need not so deeply stray,
and a face may safely lose its way.

Knocking at a Hollow Door

The hard *click* of his own door
surprised him as he stepped into
the soft-rugged hallway.
After whirling toward the sound,
he stopped and stared.
He couldn't quite understand about doors anymore.
Damn it, did they go in or out?
Did some go in and others go out?
Could you tell somebody
which kind you'd like to order?
Why couldn't he have just
an *in* door or an *out* door?

His son had put him here, in this place,
wherever this was.
He wasn't quite sure where he was,
or *when* he was where he was or wasn't.
And what the hell was going *on*, here?
From inside a moment incomplete,
he stared outward—at the door—
staring and staring from where he stood in the hallway,
wondering, with greater confusion,
where he was or wasn't.
Then, the fingers of that frozen hand
slowly curled into desperate request.
And there he stood, knocking on a hollow door,
asking the emptiness to let him in.

Such a Rain

By the window she stood, with the lights turned out,
to watch the rain.
The drops had become words that still seemed falling
from a very inclement doctor's visit.
She wished the rain could bathe itself.
Yes, perhaps the rain could wash the words
and make them fall down, cleaned.
She wished it could be such a rain,
that could the black sky attenuate,
until propitious colors might appear again
and brighter words seem more to fall from dreams.
Who needed a sky all black?
She wished that she could give it back,
and order a different one to watch.
But, the wrong sky had formed;
so, now, her very last hope for a clearer sky
could only come with the rain.
Alone, in silence, to the drops,
she watched the words come down.
Yes, the rain would have to wash itself,
to clean this last chance for a very good day.
So, she wished there might be miracle things,
and she wished that this were such a rain—
that could even wash its own storm away.

The Portrait

Her body had settled into a posture of prayer,
still fully dressed after returning to her apartment,
kneeling at her walker before a small lamp stand
in her bedroom.

It almost looked as if she were
about to pray
over the lamp stand and out the window,
to send words of gratitude toward heaven.
Yet, hands remained unfolded and fingers loose,
with the arms stretched forward,
draped straight across each side of her walker,
as though slapped into place and left there, unmoved,
for, in fact, her entire being had been left there,
unable to move,
after the surprise of a fall from tenuous balance.

Of all ironies,
she could see herself in a stand-up mirror
that leaned against the wall.
She had always hated that—
to see herself for very long,
even in a photograph.
Now, she had to look at herself
congealed as the subject,
posed in the wrong portrait.
So passionately did she wish to rise—
off her aching knees and back to herself unfallen.
She tried and tried, with no result,
then glanced, once more, while almost cursing,
to see her image in its pose of kneeling.
What cruelty had left her looking
like she was praying and giving thanks?

continued

Once more she tried so hard to rise,
but she both failed and resaw her portrait in the mirror.
They looked so much alike—
failure in the falling and giving thanks on bended knee.
Slowly, she closed her eyes, as two tears
journeyed down a wrong portrait,
fallen from similarities.

The Maybe Sky

Wheels slowed with tender worry at the speed bump,
then gently conquered that small mountain of resistance
to the parallel rise and fall of a solo grunt
as gray hair neatly arranged in a bun
above a cream-colored, silky blouse
and a full, black skirt
bent into a physical push
against the weight of the wheelchair,
black, old-fashioned shoes following in the
tracks of this trek over the obstacle.
With concern, she glanced down,
at the pallid, blank face beneath a baseball cap,
then glanced upward again, into the ephemeral feel of the sky,
before eyes returned to imperative,
looking farther down the remains of the way
he would ride and she, abide.

She had taken her memories out for a walk;
yet, while feet of fidelity trod upon remembrance,
all she released wandered into the sky.
Maybe there wasn't pain up ahead;
maybe a spouse who could only babble, now,
still formed wonderful thoughts, deep inside;
maybe they weren't left on the side of the road
like refugees from a lost war with time,
but neared some horizon, new and bright,
that they didn't know about.
Maybe it would stop feeling hard
and there'd be an end to the fright—
a fragile smile released upward, on its trembling,
to float into the blue palette—
because…
a person could read signs in a maybe sky,
where the clouds could look like *anything*.

Gaspings

He goes tethered to his oxygen—
heard before seen, coming down the hall
of the retirement complex:
desperate sucking sounds
in a confusing, alarming approach of noise,
other-worldly.
The oxygen canister rattles
in his walker
as he approaches,
plastic tubes ascending
from a compressed, expensive sky
which he must buy;
and, as the sky
goes into his nose,
frightened eyes dart down for a quick moment
to wonder how much good weather
may be left inside.

Appropriate Attire

She had consciously thought that a lover of irony
would assume this to be a golden moment,
so meticulously had she aspired to appearance
for the concert this evening,
in the retirement center's great room, downstairs.
So very diligently had she labored on her hair,
then her make-up,
surely choosing just the right rouge and lipstick, in the end,
and, finally, just the right shoes
to coordinate ultimate salience —
but, the great guarantor had been the gown,
beyond all doubt: the champion of the attire.

Well…the concert was about to begin, downstairs.
Opening notes would float out and rise just right, probably,
and all of the audience would sparkle
from the garments of their good taste—
yes, sparkle from appropriate attire.
But, she?
Well—inching beyond the toppled walker,
grunt by grunt, moan by moan, frustrated sob by sob, tear by tear,
with her hair exploded out of arrangement
and her make-up running, after the impact of the fall,
struggling to reach the lifeline string on the distant wall
for tonight's special event of her own,
crawling across the living room floor in an evening gown,
she…had turned out to be decidedly overdressed.

Chablis and the River Lee

Aberrations of the night
arrive by sudden narration
—voiced from the two-way radio
or from the phone at the receptionist's desk—
engendering a jolt of stiffened concentration,
then a hurry down the hall that way,
which turns into a thickening avenue of tension
toward an alarm of amorphous looming.

"Security! You're needed in 244—*immediately!*"
And off I rushed, into B-wing,
passkeys jingling in a nervous theme song.

After a fast, arriving knock,
and an even quicker twist of key,
I let the safety of my own essence fall
out of the prelude hall,
into what dread might wait;
yet, all I could see
was the gentlest of smiles,
sent from a wheelchair, up at me,
and a bottle of wine in wait.
Then, a small voice rose with our exigency:
"Can you pull out the cork for me?"

Although hands seemed too gnarled
to hold on tight,
I recognized the soul:
a passionate wish to still reside
here, on the independent side.

As I looked down, toward her wish,
I saw us not only there, where we seemed,
but in my old Cork of Ireland,

in an Irish shebeen.
We were both there and *else*where,
at a lower case and an upper case C,
when the cork pulled free;
and, for one night more, she sailed past her stress—
on chablis and the River Lee.

Echoes of Yesteryear

Perhaps the stool had edged forward just right,
measuring itself into formality.
Perhaps there had followed that proper, dramatic pause
for an invitation to the Muses,
then a hush of sweet anticipation
throughout the intimate concert hall,
making the silence pulsate.

Perhaps both lovely hands had upward arced,
then artfully poised at apex,
bent at the wrist,
before impelled descent
for the shattering of the silence,
when ten fingers spread and struck as one—
heard *just* by one…as I,
the lone member of the audience,
passed by outside, in chance patrol,
strolling the retirement complex halls.

Yet, while one hand stilled
my would-be discordant keys,
the other hand motioned in lonely applause.
Privileged, I walked
through the beauty of invisible notes
from that apartment
while the hall filled with
echoes of yesteryear

Ghost in the Parking Lot

Wheels—they could roll you away.
They could roll you far away from before,
toward the great, unwonted way.
And while newness formed in your windowpanes,
you could travel out of never, into maybe.
A cane and two worn, leather shoes
tapped and shuffled closer,
then stopped in the empty, asphalt rectangle,
one imagined car-length from the curb.
Yes, there it was, the number of his parking space;
and, there was his name, still painted on the curb,
although soon the name of another would replace his
to loom there in fresh paint,
and he'd even be able to *smell* the name!

He had grown too old, they said, to be out on the road.
Funny, how long, long ago, he had been too young!
He thought back to when his age had turned exactly right.
How sweet it had proven, how sweetly enabling.
With the car, he'd become more than himself;
now, they'd returned his capacity to that of a lesser being.
In a way, after all the miles, he had driven himself to irony.
Well…old, yes.
But he would not act like an old grump about it.
He would face this unique moment with basic dignity,
and appreciate the journey made,
every thrill once felt at the pictures of life
which came into view through the windowpanes.
He stared toward where the car used to be,
seeing it only in memory.
But, before turning away from what was not,
he smiled toward a ghost in the parking lot.

The Prelude Pause

How things had changed,
to now receive life's information through his *derrière*—
for, at landing's first touch, he could *feel* the coming truth,
with panic transporting happiness away,
then rushing throughout his being
in an attack of foreknowledge.
This was supposed to be such a tranquil moment:
sweet closure on the day's long transpirings
and the requirement of mind's parallel labor.
All of day and self would be blessed with ending.
But, he had figured it wrong, this day's arithmetic.
There had turned out to be a remainder:
one event left in the calculation of the day.
And, now, he was in that torment unique
of a happening's prelude pause.

Having pushed backward, off his walker,
to say good night to day,
too little of his age-cursed rump
had landed on the mattress—
denied solidity, granted only the precarious.
Of all ironies, he had been a mechanical engineer,
and, during his career, had actually done a few great things.
How lessened had become the capacities.
Time's theft of most leg strength seemed particularly frustrating.
Now, theory of leverage ended at theory.
Slowly, he began to slide out of the prelude pause,
off the edge of the bed,
knowing he would fall to the floor,
from which he'd be unable to rise—
cognizant that he would find himself compelled, then,
to push the lifeline button around his neck to beckon help.

How reduced he'd become.
How sickening and how maddening!
And how…humiliating.
After a lifetime of high competence,
he had failed at going to bed.

Flying

In contemplative rhythm,
the metal walker rolled out of the evening hallway,
through pulled-back, double doors,
into the high viewing-room of the world outside.
Slowly, across the retirement center rug,
wheels performed their cycle,
approaching a wall of windows.
Even from only part of the way there
she could see the ubiquitous stream
of red lights on the highway,
easily viewable through a thin veil of trees,
their symbolic forest.
Flickering, red, brake beams and glistening white light
mixed into mobile, modern art
that kept going and going
in a portrayal of endlessness.
Yet, she turned from the panorama,
lowering her head as she neared the glass,
as if aware of the terms of invisibility
finally offered to her, for sharing, by the hosting air.

When wheels slowed in their turning,
then stopped at the precipice,
she let her head, lowered, in that silence stay.
She knew she should beg it not to be there—
the end of the way.
She should surrender reason,
and beg the precipice to undo its looming;
she should fill with fright and beg for mercy.
Yet, long did life-thought hover,
without any sound at all,
in the final space
that touched the third-floor window-wall,
until, abruptly, her hands, old, but still adroit,
tightened on walker handles

to slam it hard against the base,
like an exclamation point…
while her eyes slowly dared to lift
over the edge of time.
So what, if the way had ended?
So what, if the allotment of dirt had run out
for a trail that exists up ahead?
So what, if she had arrived
where a person is supposed to capitulate?
Just…look at how far she had come!
Why on earth should, now, she cry
when she had pushed her old and faithful walker
all the way down to the trail's goodbye…
then all the way up to the sky?

A Burning Desire

Well, how was *she* supposed to know,
in these modern times,
how warm *warm* was?
Besides, all she had wanted to do
was have a relaxing moment.
Isn't that what you're *supposed* to do
at the end of a day?
The security guard will probably tell everyone
who did it.
They didn't need to know!
No, they didn't need to know
she'd pressed minutes instead of seconds;
and, they didn't need to know
she'd gone into the living room to watch television
and forgotten about it,
while the whole procedure was taking place.
All over one little apple!
So what?
Big deal!
Big deal, that her relaxing moment had caught fire.
Big deal, that her apartment's smoke detector had gone off.
Big deal, that she had opened her door and
all the smoke had billowed into the retirement complex hall.
Big deal, that it had set off the *whole fire alarm!*
So she didn't know how to use the microwave—
so what?
Big deal!
Well, *let* them know who did it,
because even if they were mad,
they'd sure have to give her credit
and admit one thing:
although *she* hadn't ended up with a nice, warm apple…
for minutes, not seconds, she had
brought a hot time to the ol' complex tonight!

Gliding

Slowly, his head lost its tilt,
sinking so low at the night, library reading table
that his eyes slid off the spread newspaper,
vision left to dangle, finally,
in mists of void.
Funny, how good it felt—to be gliding.
Why should he stay here,
in these retirement confines,
all the time, when…
As ignored light from the solitary reading lamp
glistened off his bent, bald head,
he crawled into the cockpit of his mind,
and let himself…*soar!*
Up he felt himself snap,
initially bobbing behind the lead plane
at the end of the cable,
then…*released*…
to glide, like a new, free star,
through the earth's dominion.
Wondrous it felt,
to float through abeyance above the planet,
to join life's suspension,
and magic-carpet ride high above all constraints.
He could stay up there forever!
Up, up he went, above it all—
above the planet and above the years:
gliding, again, in his 1940s uniform
over Nazi-held Europe,
fighting Hitler,
or gliding somewhere peaceful,
somewhere else—
somewhere, maybe farther…
or, somewhere, maybe nearer…
or…hell, just *gliding*.

Holding Starlight

It was love that reached my ears—
"We're going out to look at the sky!"—
harmonizing with the sound of
opening, retirement center double doors,
as my gaze, rising from the security desk,
perceived two smiling people holding hands
exit our artificial light
to attend a special exhibit of art,
hung high in the gallery of the night.
On display was a rare phenomenon,
a night beyond the normal sky,
for Mars had arced close enough to ally
her sparkle's descent with ours
and thicken the stellar cascade.
Grounded on Earth, these lovers
upward gazed through the vast exhibition hall,
then reached for the gift of artspell's fall.
Two hands wrapped around
their part of the night,
then tried to hold starlight.

The Follow Place

Toward the lure of sound
he rose from his stuffed chair in the high,
retirement apartment,
pulled by unintended invitation
to send his contemplations
through the window frame.
Easily, he spotted the mower below;
then, vision shifted—
pensively, slowly—
to lock, at last, just behind that figure…
and stare into the emptiness there.

Miles of grass ago
he had been the mower,
when that spot behind had not been empty,
but filled with vivacity and unconditional accompaniment,
when a collie's smile, with barks melodic,
had gone 'round and 'round with him in the patterns,
wherever the curves might lean,
on lanes of lowered green.
Into the emptiness, now, did he stare,
as if choosing to wait for what was not there.

Then, he shook his head, as if wounded by time.
What was he doing?
It was silly, wondering like this.
What dog could rise from memory
to bark and run through time's wall?
Then was then, now lost.
It was silly, so silly, even wondering—
even sensing the impulse.
Yet…he could hear that sound,
the sound of the mower,
a sound that made the wall fall down;

continued

and—he couldn't help it—
before he confirmed, with a turn,
logic from the window,
he smiled quiet rebellion against the expected,
and let a last glance chance a fall through the space
to envision a wish toward the follow place.

A Ladder Not Long Enough

Was it too much to ask?
She *liked* being quiet.
No, she never complained;
she *preferred* a low profile, but...
when a problem finally grew out of hand
in this retirement place,
couldn't she, just for once, ask them
to do something about it?
After all, even if her kids handled her checkbook now,
she paid a lot of money to stay here.
Surely, she could lodge her very first complaint!
So, why wouldn't the people who run this place
just go ahead and fix it?
It didn't make sense.
Didn't they want to make sense?
Why didn't they just do something about it,
and *stop* those things up there,
those things she had told them about?
Was it too much to ask?
Couldn't they just send some workers,
who could bring a ladder that was long enough
to reach what she told them was wrong?
How many times had she phoned about this?
But, no! They *still* hadn't done anything about them!
They were still there, in the hall,
right outside her apartment door—
up, up, yes, *up there*, high:
all those *voices in the ceiling!*
Couldn't they remove them?
Couldn't they just bring a ladder that was long enough?

The Other Side of the Window

It had looked so bizarre:
smoke's rise, in escape, through the unused grills.
Then, a slowly retracted oven door,
like a theater curtain opening,
staged its ballet in conflagrant orange,
with flamed undulations that threatened to burn
the uncolored parts of night.
Nitrogen-pressurized tight,
from the nearest recess in the hallway wall,
the extinguisher offered a chemical cloud
to censure such choreography.
Yet, irony, too, can rise in the night,
for, the spray that had ended the orange ballet
now floated into complicity,
to join the smoke it had made
while suppressing such burning dance…
both floating, suddenly, back, toward me,
as a new and junctured entity
—a pair of confluent clouds—
stealing all air as it came!
To the window I managed to retreat,
desperately raising the frame—
to posture there with nose pressed to the screen,
toward the other sovereignty.
How I wanted the other side of the window,
with its separate invisibility,
for the first time knowing,
as I breathed it toward me,
just how beautiful the unseen can be.

Partner in the Dark

They had night-breathed so rhythmically
that only a single exhale
had seemed travel across the bedroom.
Preferring feel to sight,
they had fit so well inside the dark
there'd been no need for light.
She'd always had this side, he that,
as they'd blended day's-end whisperings
to duet a passage into sleep
upon the road to dreams.
Now, she remained with what the night might seem,
for light revealed her left alone, no one for whom to wait.
But, once again, sweet night had come,
and she could dream before she'd sleep.
Across night's bed could breathe her whispers,
the echoes another's voicing seem,
and one be two, without the light,
and solo be duet in dream.
So, inside night, where the light had fallen,
she turned on the half that was her part
to whisper alone and sweetly feel
her partner in the dark.

Too Far Away

Well, where the heck *was* it?
Why couldn't he remember where he'd parked the darn thing?
It was funny, how so many of them
had decals on their rear bumpers.
It made all the cars look like billboards!
No, he wouldn't glue any sticker onto his car's bumper,
but…where *was* his car?
Had he parked somewhere past where he remembered?
Had he parked…too far away?
Legs that had grown stiff and performed only short steps, now,
resumed exploration through the back parking lot
of the senior living complex.
Holding his apartment door key,
as if it would start the car,
in tiniest steps he explored space to space,
voyaging the asphalt as light left the day;
but, he'd parked it so many years away
that his eyes could not focus enough to see
a car that used to be.

Made in Heaven

From the security guard desk,
that unusually late-hour return to the retirement complex
should have apprised me of a theme of greater reach.
Indeed, there did accompany her entrance
quite a symbol of surprise,
portraying her arrival beyond a normal ingress:
a silver crown, no less, pronged high in the silver hair.
Regathering myself from the unorthodox,
I selected quick salutation: "Oh, you're a queen!"
However, I had aimed too low,
there, at mere bonds of earth,
for, as the ornate, double doors closed behind her,
she tilted her silver crown and her silver hair and her smile
correctingly higher.
Yes, higher and higher went all three,
way, way, *way* beyond the throne—
"I'm not a queen!"—
tilting ever upward to edit my script,
until, looking toward higher sky only she could see,
through a smile made in heaven, she rewrote the last line:
"I'm a *goddess!*"

The Empty Chair

"They've taken her to the other side,"
he explained to me, the security guard
who had brought her medicine, as usual,
from the pharmacy delivery.
In his independent living apartment,
he spoke, seated, from an old, stuffed chair
while a forefinger pointed to its match,
a chair partnered to his,
suddenly empty.
"Sorry you had to come all this way, but today…
today they came to wheel her"
—with a head nod toward the other half of the complex—
"over there."
While the finger kept pointing,
we both stared at the empty chair,
until the sad voice, like the voice of fate,
sent an exhale into the air,
that slowly traveled from chair to chair,
then dispersed in the emptiness there.

The Night Unwritten

These gusts of dusk cannot be dissuaded from their mystery.
Invisible they stay, and intangible,
refusing to foretell
the genre of the night unwritten.
In such blankness,
they allow the fears to rise;
comes, once again, slowly, a nocturnal tale
that may prove either fair or furied.

As solitary guard within this setting,
I wish I could expunge
all scenes ill-blown while night may remain uncome.
I stare fervently into the exhale I feel
gusted across this prelude.
But these early gusts will not reveal
what may or not be scripted.
That which may loom sojourns well hidden,
and the night remains unwritten.

A Little Flower Song

It was the talk of the complex,
how much they must have spent
to render the entrance of this retirement center
more *flourished* than the entrances of their competitors—
surely, the entire Marketing Department budget,
maybe *beyond!*
Flowers rose up *every*where, outside,
embellishing the area of the entrance—
this kind of flower, that kind, and maybe even new hybrids;
and, certainly, all had better stay alive and beautiful and untouched
during all the length of spring and summer,
because those brand new flowers were, literally,
the entire show of the marketing minds this fiscal year—
soft, bright magnets to attract potential, new, rich residents.
Smiles dominated the faces of the Executive Director and
the Assistant Director, and each of the Marketing Visages,
as they and current residents stood excitedly in the lobby
to remark about the extravaganza outside,
which embellished the entrance in so many colors,
and, indeed, had cost a bundle—*thousands*—and had better last
all spring and summer, standing tall through those months,
untouched, like some great and elegant advertisement.

Silence arrived in lobby-wide unison
as the tell-tale, double doors opened
to admit a reentering resident—
all eyes snap-descending onto what the hands on the walker
also held as the resident returned inside,
cheerfully humming to herself,
a happy song invisibly dancing above her new possessions,
for she had enjoyed an excellent morning.
She had pushed her walker, step by step, outside
to see what the day might bring;
and, now, she was returning, with what, in fact, it had brought:

a pair of lovely bouquets,
one for each hand!
What a wonderful day, to have discovered beautiful flowers,
and, in the loveliness of surprise, to have *picked a bunch!*

Slowly, she worked her way through the crowd,
through the frozen figures of fellow residents, the Executive Director,
the Assistant Director, and the open-mouthed, Marketing types—
swaying step by step past all the silent, staring looks,
to reach the elevator, whose button she pushed.
Then, in a moment, she entered it;
and, as the elevator door rhythmically closed,
the stunned and silent mass shot their last look
at two really beautiful bouquets…
and heard the happy humming
of a little flower song.

Cry from a Separate Solitude

"*Help* me!"—squeezed into its share of the air
on this healthcare floor of fragile thinking,
that verbal breath hitting my face
as I rushed into the chaos.
Hurrying words down,
toward that frail and wheelchaired suppliant,
I sought to offer humane relief,
for her to know that because another
on this floor of mental fragility
had confusedly pulled the alarm,
not peril, but *illusion*, sounded now:
a fiction in their living place.
But, as I resumed imperative haste,
behind me ascended her cry's reprise—
"*Help* me!"—
as if I had uttered no answer at all
when I'd walked through her words in the hall.

As I deepened into disorientation,
high chaos forced my own mind's decline
toward the level of this floor.
Surprised not to discern the alarm box key
from the unclipped ball of so many choices,
private alarm passed through me, as I passed through this hall;
and, I silently wished, among all the noises,
for clarity to be brief anomaly
within the wild discord.
Then, I spotted the key
carved to end the spell of chaos.

With a thankful twist came tranquility's return,
allowing my own return through the hall,
appreciating the general and gentle fall
of the residents back into stillness.

Yet, near the last exit, I heard, from behind,
out of the quiet, that cry's reprise:
"Help me!"
Then, my mistake I realized.
I had thought it had risen out of the scene.
But, from where no one could reach, from private mystery too deep,
it had been disparate to that discord.
It remained in its own fall of quietude,
for it had not been a voice in the dissonance,
but a cry from a separate solitude.

The Silver Derby

How the aroma of grass would waft up
as the smell of the summer day
they galloped through!
They could make the nearby world shake
as sprays of dirt and dust
flew off the kick of hoofs;
and, wind that rushed through
mane and rider's hair
meant even the invisible
welcomed them there.

He stared meaningfully into the remembrance air,
listening to precious echoes.
Then, he returned to the moment that he inhabited,
for it was just another, fine night
at the Silver Derby,
down in the game room
of the retirement center range.
With skills of the past,
he settled more appropriately
into the saddle of his fold-up chair;
then, hands that had once held reins
gave a quick, no-nonsense, signaling snap…
and out toppled the dice,
clicking across the card table
like a burst of hoofs.

Going Nowhere

He had turned into a paradox:
something that *descended* inside an elevator, rising.
In the magical days,
he could have balanced on one leg the whole way up
as the elevator had risen through the chute,
past all the floors.
Time had given him that much strength.
Now, time, following its own sense of balance,
had taken that strength away.
Now, he rose through the chute
lying foolishly on the elevator floor,
exactly where he'd fallen
after pushing the top floor button,
then turning too fast.
Even the balance of his cane
had not provided enough compensation.
Now, both he and the cane lay at the bottom
as the elevator rose to the top.

Of course, he had pressed the lifeline button under his shirt;
but, as his own descent ascended,
changing from level to level in this retirement complex,
how could they know where he was?
And, in truth, the way he felt,
as his floor-held body uselessly altered
from floor to floor to floor…
actually, he wasn't anywhere, at all.
He could fall, but he could not rise.
But, it was okay.
He might be down, going up,
and might be moving, going nowhere.
Yet, thanks to the counsel of the years,
he was able, now—
able to be true underneath the false body,
able to take a beating without losing himself…
able to collect invisible scars.

Blendings

What was *wrong* with him?
What was happening to his brain?
And why did he feel so…so *strange*?
Maybe he should call his wife out here to the kitchen,
from the other room, but…
he had always been the stable one, the one to take care of things.
Yet, now, suddenly…
he was the one who felt so…
so different…
so, uh…*lightheaded.*
This was, uh…a, uh…uh, uh…
sensation he had never…felt before.
It was so odd to, uh…feel a new way…at his age.
My God, what the hell…*was* this?
It almost felt like…the *end* of him!

Almost as something with which to fiddle during the disorientation,
his fingers stretched from the kitchen chair
to the nearby shelf where all their medications stood,
like the pair of them, through thick or thin: two together.
But, as his eyes stared downward at the recently used pill bottle,
the greatest jolt of panic, yet, ascended into prominence
within this strange malaise:
he had not swallowed his normal pills—
but had swallowed, irretrievably, into the core of himself…
hers!
Into his being had passed the essence of her medicinal world!
Now, those potent, anti-psychotic chemicals
were melting into his own inner life, which had vowed
"'til death do us part!"

He had survived so many crises through the years.
Lord, could he make it through *this* one?
"For better or for worse," they had pledged;
yes, "'til death do us part" had they promised.

Indeed, had they shared the way—
hand in hand, and heart to heart.
Now, they had added *drug to drug!*
Well, through this night, as never before,
together they would go—
for, uh…uh, for…better or for worse…
'til, uh…death would them part…might them part…
this night together, as, uh…all nights had been…
the two of them…
melting together…
into blendings.

Last Friend

His walker wheels worked their way down the hall
in slow, plaintive rhythm,
while he with head of thinning white hair
traveled, bent, above the handles,
lost in last images.
He thought about life, verdant, at summer's exit,
with its capitulation into brown,
then its exit from the visible,
lost beneath the snow,
just as final colored leaf and most loyal limb
must prove divisible,
and the light of day, each night, must go.
He thought of sunsets fading into dark of void,
and shooting stars that arc away,
and the calendar page that must be turned
at closure of its final day.
But, most of all, he thought about
the notice he had seen,
taped to the elevator wall,
which apprised him that laughter, too, can end,
for, in elegant print and with floral borders,
it apprised him that…
he had just lost his last friend.

In Mid-Air

Lord, his physique no longer resided on the ground,
but was *actually in mid-air!*
By the way the appendages flailed and flopped,
his three hundred-pound body had seemingly
converted into the poor excuse for an *airplane:*
flying on a wing and a prayer!
What a crew it was that had aspired to lift him
off his motorized scooter and into bed,
after the discovery that his legs had finally
become too shot to help,
like parts now worn out and no longer kept in stock.
All regular-hours workers had left for the day;
and, now, there they were, with their desperate grunting and struggling,
the only crew left on the runway, thrown together from the night people:
the straining nurse from Venezuela;
the small-statured Hispanic trainee, having arrived early,
on the city bus's last run,
with no car of his own;
and the Irish security guard,
big but mostly over the hill.

Lord, he'd started to *tilt!*
His right leg, in the grips of the nurse and trainee,
was not rising as fast as the left leg;
and, now, he'd started to travel through the air *slightly sideways!*
But, they couldn't put just *half* of him to bed!
"Hey, the Irish guy's the only one lifting me!"—
he sputtered in a sort of *Mayday.*
Worse, despite the fact the crew had begun to physically *shake*
in the effort to prove themselves hydraulic,
all ascent seemed to be losing momentum,
even the left leg.

continued

How could this pathetic scenario have developed
in the life of a former heavyweight wrestler,
a strongman who used to pin down all challenges
until somebody counted to three?
How could this *be*—to have turned into
the facsimile of some old airplane,
flying tilted in mid-air,
and now on the verge of losing altitude?
Lord, was he going to *crash?*

Ironically, the unorthodox flight had ascended
close enough to the bed's level to actually tease them.
But, the nurse/trainee motor on his big, right leg
had definitely stalled, just below success,
which left only the big, left leg tilt-shaking higher.
Well, here was his wing; now, where was the prayer?
Even the left had slowed so much, now, trying to quiver upward,
that it seemed they *all* were going to fall out of the sky!
But, just as he imagined the pain of being dropped,
the left side once more began to rise, as though on a miracle wind—
almost there, almost high enough—
until…the barest portion of that one enormous buttock
slapped onto the bedtop's runway!
Then, with an erupting trio of wild grunts from the night crew,
buttock number two touched down.
Soon, as grunts and fear of falling
announced the airport closed for end of the day,
the last crew on for the last plane extinguished the last landing
light,
while a salvaged mass of wing and prayer
slowly taxied down a bed top runway,
out of mid-air and into good night.

Leaf Rain

Some European critics had originally belittled Robert Frost
as "a rural American poet," but...
she was *glad* she'd been a teacher who'd taught
how his eyes had searched for beauty.
Even now, as her own last page turned,
his spirit instilled life with a special thrill:
to stare out this retirement apartment window
at the tiny, symbolic woods, made of trees beside the highway,
in search of earth's poetic feel.
Of course, it'd become harder to spot inspiration,
looking through eyes so old.
Yet, just as she felt an impulse of depression,
a sudden gust surprised the trees,
which began to lose old leaves.
Down they swirled so beautifully,
baring the limbs to beckon leaves new,
that they wind-danced into ending's art
as "rural American poetry" beside the urban roar.
She thanked the little woods for the gift that it had given—
that she could see their poem
and watch the beauty of an ending,
falling in a leaf rain.

Final Applause

He stood tallest among the many in the elevator
as it rose back to their apartments
after the performance in the
retirement complex concert hall.
His full, white hair hovered over all their heads,
still topping the straight posture
from so many years as an officer.
And, as they ebulliently released
their glowing critiques of the performance,
just minutes ago concluded, he, taller
and dignified, merely nodded,
and merely smiled,
as if, perhaps, he loomed above them
in other statures, as well.

Like an officer and a gentleman,
he held the OPEN button for all of them to exit,
then stepped out last.
Yet, a few steps from the closing door,
he seemed to hesitate,
then turned to face the echo of his exit,
staring at the ending
until the elevator returned with
more post-entertainment, third-floor faces.
A smiling woman with a walker exited and
wheeled toward him on the way to her apartment:
"Did you enjoy the show?"
Although straight posture held in place,
his face beneath the high, white hair
seemed to yield to loss:
"Oh, was there a *show* downstairs?
I…must have missed it."
Her smile diminished, somewhat, in confusion:
"Oh, I thought I saw you down there.
Weren't you at the show?"

Standing tall above the certainty:
"No, uh…I guess I didn't see that show yet."

As the third-floor crowd shuffled smilingly down the hall,
in an aura of remembrance,
the lone, dignified man, dressed for an occasion,
stared into the empty elevator,
then stepped inside its vacancy
before the door could close.
He stood where he had stood before,
still the tallest in the elevator,
although now in a crowd of one.
Then, as the door slowly closed, he
standing straight in his separate stature,
began privately to descend
toward the start of a show
that had already reached its end.

The Dream Pendant

Well, the legs were finally gone—
the legs she'd worked so hard to keep
to stay in independent living.
Once fully cognizant the directors grew,
she, like neighbors they'd watched decline,
would find herself gone, too—
moved to the healthcare half,
yes, the dreaded "other side"…
where life begins to end.
How she'd fought and fantasized about staying away!
All those excruciating therapy routines
she had strained her spirit into,
when she would wear her mask against the pain
and smile instead of cry!
Just moments ago, from the bed, her arm had
stretched toward the lamp stand for some small thing,
yet found only irony,
as she'd felt everything slip away.
If only her legs could have stiffened,
and her toes dug in!
How she had begged them to,
but they could no longer answer…
and, during that silence,
sliding farther and farther,
she had felt her independent life
cruelly fly away.
In the culminating irony,
she'd fallen into a wedge between the mattress side
and the metal handle attached to the frame!
She'd stuck there as a flying rag doll,
in mid-air at the side of her bed—
neither up nor down,
frozen into falling.

So, there she, unmoving, flew through the sky,
toppled over the edge, yet remaining in air,
left merely to dangle in a frozen lean
as a suspended symbol of her own dream.

Tilted Sadness

From behind,
the thin back in the wheelchair
could be seen in full paroxysm—
the cloth of that old, white robe
loosening during each incipient heave,
then abruptly stretched tight.
As I neared, bringing more of her into sight,
I saw that she sat slightly bent
over a figure of her lament.
Yet, when we were finally side by side,
with a downward glance, I realized
that on some sharp curve along life's way,
her emotions had tilted too far,
and had lost their definition,
for the wounded being upon her lap,
which she obsessively stoked
and cried over,
turned out to be, although real to her,
softness sewn in the shape of a cat—
tears landing on a toy.
From beyond her, glancing back,
I discerned no more than what remained there:
only tilted sadness,
traveling last miles in an old wheelchair.

Night Talk

He shuffled in stocking feet
toward the old, worn dresser
to slowly open the top drawer,
reach carefully inside with two hands,
then delicately carry an extracted garment
all the way across the room toward the bed,
those slow steps accompanied by solo-voicings:
"I had beef tips and broccoli for dinner—pretty good.
I couldn't resist blue cheese dressing
on the salad tonight.
Probably bad for my cholesterol, I know.
But I ate it, anyway."
Ever so gently did he lower the garment
onto one side of the bed, left it at rest,
while stocking feet shuffled
to the other side.

He opened another dresser drawer
to extract pajamas.
His trousers fell to the rug—
he picked them up, with a grunt, then folded
them over the back of a stuffed chair.
"And I picked a fruit cup for dessert.
I was a good boy, there."
Trembling, his stretching fingers managed to
hook and toss off his socks
arm braced by the dresser;
then, his shirt joined the trousers
in their landing spot across the chair.
The bedroom soliloquy continued,
while pajamas carefully replaced day's apparel:
"It had all kinds of things in it—seedless grapes and
little, red cherries and…all kinds of stuff."

continued

With a small burst and second grunt,
now barefoot and pajama-clad, he
resumed ambulation,
shuffling toward a small, corner table
covered with beautiful bottles.
In a wonted way, his hands pursued familiarity there,
pouring into an old, carved glass:
"I'm going to…fix myself…
a…big…bad…glorious…wonderful…
vodka tonic!"

Soon, balancing the glass, pajama-clad,
he crawled into bed without a splash.
The sound of a long sip preceded the turning
of a left-behind, lonely head
toward the empty, pink nightgown,
postured where it had always been during her living years:
"Good night, my one and only, " he whispered tenderly.
"You know I still love you—don't you, dear?"

Slipped from the Window

All these new do-dads and the todayness
made him uneasy.
Even though it was slowing, now, to pull into
its official retirement center space,
to bring them back from dialysis,
he still couldn't even recognized half of the darned gadgets
in this big car.
There was nothing but *new* stuff inside!
All this *todayness*, he couldn't get used to it.
It was just not as comfortable as yesterday.
All these gadgets, they…didn't match his memories.
Why couldn't he just grab a knob, like he used to,
and roll down the window—
yes, and roll it *hard*, if he were in the mood,
to lower it fast…
or roll it slowly, and just a little,
if he only wanted the breeze to slip inside,
through a crack in the top,
so he could feel it in his hair?
And it should be the person *at that window*
who should decide to roll it up or down,
not the *driver!*
Why should the *driver* be able to roll somebody else's window
up or down?
And certainly not with a *button!* A button should never be able
to roll a window up or down, at all!
It should only be a *knob!*

Yes, the driver grew a little peeved
—just now, just as he started to get out of the car—
because someone yelled: "Hey, you forgot to turn the lights off!"
So what, if even he, himself, had forgotten, again, that
the doggone car turns its own lights off?
The driver is supposed to have to remember that, not the car!
A car shouldn't even be able to turn its own lights off!

continued

So, other people shouldn't get mad.
But, worst of all, management shouldn't have laughed.
They shouldn't have laughed when he'd put his idea
into the official suggestion box.
Just because nobody had ever done such a thing,
why couldn't *they* still do it?
Didn't it make sense?
Wouldn't it solve everything that was wrong with this todayness?
It was an absolutely problem-solving suggestion:
just trade in these new cars for *old* cars!
They shouldn't have laughed,
then left everyone stuck with todayness.
All the old comfort had completely disappeared, maybe out the
crack.
Yes, the guy, who was already mad,
must have used his improper button
to sneak the pane down a little way, then had left it open too long,
because, as anyone now could see,
the whole thing was all gone:
yesterday had fallen out the window
and the memories had blown away.

The Thinning Dark

The great noise of a neighborhood being built
had driven him from the trees—
the exact, same noise which had irritated me, as well,
while I, as security guard, had foot-patrolled
the large, circling, asphalt road
that bounded the healthcare/retirement complex.
That vast complex loomed always to my left, as I walked,
while the dark mystery of the trees—*his* trees—
loomed always to the right:
two disparate sovereignties allowed by the size of night.
But, the woods had been sold from far away;
and, abruptly, the only host to stay
was the linger of the thinning dark.

One by one, I recalled, another tree fell,
to develop a lessening of the once great sight
wherein two realms could dwell.
Now, the dichotomy could not be held.
Now, there he was; and, here was I—
actually looking into each other's eyes.
The ellipses of our domains had, at last, been contracted
into a junctured touch.
Yet, although I felt surprise,
I really wished the fox well,
regretting that his world had shrunken so
that we had actually met.
Each of us had frozen, and even the moment seemed still,
as if the night had stopped for us, in wait.
That the ellipses of our domains had finally junctured
I could not celebrate,
but wished, instead, that he not meet demise
while the neighborhood of man rose up.

continued

I never should have seen him, nor should he have seen me;
yet, for one frozen instant, we shared overlapped realms—
he, at one end of a glance, I, at the other,
before he broke away,
toward the shrinkage of the trees.
I hope that he can survive
against all this construction,
and wish him all remaining trees
within the thinning dark.

Last Ride into Midnight

Once again, light split the black of night
while a man rode tracks backward,
out of the retirement center mailbox
in a rhythm of remembrance.
Look at it!
How swiftly it had moved, the train,
hurrying across the face of explorations.
On the train,
he'd been able to force his way into the wind,
and, behind the great beam,
enter the mystery of midnight!

He stared down at pictures and pages
but, more to re-feel than to read.
Through years he'd explored on curves of steel,
the railroad line.
Until his ticket read *End of the Line*,
on curves of steel he'd stay.
He would ride the train by memory
on tracks across the finite.
He'd say good-bye to the dark as he rushed by,
and thrill to course its final winds—
then enter the curve that led out of sight
on his last ride into midnight.

Wall of Time

He switched the walker to attack mode
as its wheels rolled across the rug
without slowing
in an ever closer approach to the elevator
until it rammed the closed, steel door—
then, shaking, withdrew, only to poise again,
then rammed the door twice more.
So, what was *wrong* with this thing,
that it didn't listen to him?
He needed to get its attention,
to correct its mistakes,
or it would just
stay in some automatic sequence of passage
that wasn't worth a damn.
A new triple-echo of collision
sounded through the retirement center hall.
Then, the bony, gray face
beneath an old, crooked baseball cap
tilted into observation.
No, his message had not been received.
It still wanted to ignore
the rhythm of his needs and plans.
It just wanted to flow the way *it* wanted to flow.
So, it was time to ram some more.
He re-cocked the walker into attack posture.
Yes, yes—more ramming would be required
against the wall of time.

The Lost Thing

I found something in the lowest hallway,
late last night.
On rare occasions, during youth, I would
find a penny in the alley I'd traverse.
During such aberrant moments,
I would halt with incredible abruptness
into a frozen balance of surprise
to wonder if I were really looking at
what my eyes seemed to discern.
Then, finally, I would reach for it…
a miracle.
As in the echo of those decades gone,
once again had I found something lost.
In fallen light, once more I halted
with incredible abruptness
into a frozen balance of surprise
to wonder if I were really looking at
what and whom my eyes seemed to discern,
there in unplanned solitude,
there in the lowest hallway of the complex.

As security guard,
I knew that lost and lonely soul not to be
a resident of the independent side;
so, looking down, toward frightened, glazed eyes,
I issued the gentle inquiry:
"Hi, may I ask your name?"
When remembrance that deep—
of who she, herself, should be—eluded her,
I chanced to see her name taped
on the side of the wheelchair.
 "They must have forgotten to wheel you back
after the entertainment tonight.
I can see you live on the healthcare side."

continued

Quickly, this time, seeking stronger posture,
her struggling face rose as high as it could
within the intangible:
"Oh, no! I don't think I *live* here.
I…I need to catch a *bus!*"
Extricating myself from the balance of surprise,
I managed to utter: "Oh. Well, okay.
I…happen to know… where the nearest stop is."
In that echo of those decades gone,
I looked at the lost being I'd found…
and improvised —
and pushed her to a substitute bus stop
on a route beyond remembrance.

Retracings

It seemed the gurney were going the wrong way,
having *entered* the complex with the supine body,
not *exiting* with her—
pushing her farther inside the building,
not pushing her out.
"Returning one!"—they had shouted,
implying her brief welcome at the hospital had run out of tenure.
Because the new ambulance team
had brought her, in error, to the retirement side,
it fell to me, the security guard,
to guide them through the structure's maze,
to the complex's healthcare half,
where they would undo themselves of her,
then return to their waiting ambulance,
still superfluously in the glow of emergency lights,
to lift carefully inside, through those back doors,
a gurney without its body.

As we fatefully rushed to "the other side,"
I glanced down, through the contradiction, toward her,
a resident who'd become a friend.
She was returning the same way she had left:
oxygen mask across her face,
eyes closed…softly moaning.
I could translate the implication:
they had cleared a hospital bed…
and had sent her back to die.
Perceiving how she was—
hearing moans in private plight—
'though I supposedly showed the way, I knew
we walked a retracing, an ending journey,
while she drifted not toward, but away.

In Someone Else's Time

His eyes, rebelling, grew vivacious above
the clear, plastic oxygen tube
permanently inserted into his nostrils.
The negativity had finally *culminated*—
thinking autobiographical thoughts
of a denizen on the down side of life.
He, suddenly, was so *sick* of it all—
sick of looking at shadows
to wonder what was in them, waiting for him.
Under the tubes, he still had a brain,
so why not transport himself *away*?
He'd tear his mind off descended symbols—
off blood pressure readings and glucose counts,
off pill boxes and plastic tubes,
off EKGs and MRIs…
and off the big darkness up ahead.

Yes, he'd tear his mind off descendent symbols,
and fill it with symbols rising—
because a cardinal could still land in an evergreen tree,
and art ignite in autumn leaves.
A rainbow could paint the sky into magic,
and a morning could come all white
from snow that had fallen all through the night.
Although it would happen for him no more,
he felt happy to know that wonders still could be.
So, he prepared to fly away in his mind.
Yes, the leaves would color and the rainbow arc
in someone else's time;
but, just as long as he could picture
what someone else could thrill to see…
that would do just fine.

The Nothing Pond

Twin trickles had commenced their streams in propitious unison—
one current, the incipient faucet flow
at the little bathroom sink
of that retirement apartment,
soon adjusted into greater surge,
such downflow splashing onto yesterday's underwear:
the soaking subject,
lying alone in the concavity, stretched across the tightened plug,
to await a simple renaissance.

Yet, too soon, the second trickle
diverged at its own sediment…
and that current of cognizance meandered away:
away, toward the living room;
away from both hearing aids, pulled out of lost comfort;
away, to a grand, stuffed chair, right in front of the T.V.,
abruptly vibrating at maximum volume;
away, through unattended time…
far from remembrance.

While the current of a face
emptied into the basin of the living room,
back, at the original site of departed cognizance,
irony seemed float like a vessel
upon the changing surface,
as liquid climbed the banks of sink shores
to ascend, at last, to the very top…
then transformed to cascade
in a run down the outer hill
of drawers and cabinet doors,
all the way to the valley of the floor,
where the water deepened everywhere—
except inside the logical offering of the tub.

continued

There, in the basin of the bathroom floor,
splashing with odd undulations higher and higher
against the walls of the empty tub,
rose the artistry of paradox,
for it was there that lost mentality slowly *created* something:
without engineering, and *in absentia*,
lost cognizance built a nothing pond…
for the lone vessel of irony to float on.

Broken Parallel

"We've lost one," fell out of my radio in a tone strangely flat.
"Security, we've lost one."
A name and a description
—with what she wore, *maybe*—
trailed out, to follow such apprising;
then, silence took everyone else away.
So, without one knowing where the other might be,
we two commenced strange journey's duet
in a broken parallel.
Somewhere and nowhere the two of us ambled,
both in today and yesteryear;
through chance up ahead and time left behind,
we both came and we went,
though never quite there and never quite here.
When, at last, in a stairwell we converged,
she stepped from the dark while I, from the light;
yet, I was not there, while she was my sight.
As we journeyed back, through some place and nowhere,
ice from her eyes that fell to our ground
showed that in our broken parallel,
she was both lost and found.

The Color of Time

She sat alone on the balcony
on her ninetieth birthday,
to watch the day age out of light.
The younger hours had been all right,
illuminating a fresher path;
yet, this had become her part of day:
the painted spell of the aftermath.
Subtlety played above her wait
until the thrilling instant when the sky
began to paint
itself with clouds not white, but pink.
So, while color deepened above her eyes,
she painted her memories, too.
As together they turned from pink into red,
she saw time seem beautiful.
She watched the high essence of the spectrum
through the offered span of time
until the arrival of night's obsequy
removed from paints their final light,
and hues folded back into the sky.
With a subtle hiss, she watched them leave;
yet, a breeze placed a smile on her face,
for, on this fine birthday, 'though only dark could she see,
she knew that the sky was still breathing.

Rain from Another Sky

Cerebral clarity in the apartment above
had clouded over, causing
an opened bathroom faucet's water
to run over the sink,
to deepen where it fell…
until a forgetful flood could form
and water travel through the floor.

In the apartment below, the cerebral sky loomed clear,
with none of life's precipitation forecast.
It should have been another lucid day.
Yet, as that resident awoke in surprise,
she found only contradiction.
It was not fair that precipitation
should come through such lucidity
from a storm she could not even see.
It was not fair that unexplainable thunder
should crack inside day's beauty.
It was not right that disturbance should prevail
in a domain of invited calm.
Yet, her chagrin tilted high, toward what she should not see
pouring through her ceiling,
for there it came in a strange fall:
rain from another sky.

Falling Out of Day

He'd become a guest of anomaly,
apprised that a day may not always follow
the forecast of assumptions.
He'd learned that contradiction
can usurp the way—
such as, when an old man hurries his walker
into the bathroom faster than he can really follow;
senses the portent of alarm
when essence tilts into precarious prelude;
then, abruptly, *falls away*, into full release—
essence hurled through transition, with a sudden twist,
to fall backward, into the wait of emptiness!
In fact, such an old man was he —
legs draped over time's side, dangling beyond extrication.
And, there, he remained, in anomalous lay,
inhabiting that vacuity—
a fully clothed man in his empty tub:
a figure who fell out of his own day.

Last Posture

Every set of nervous eyes: they were all looking at her.
Funny, how she hadn't flopped off her chair,
to end up lying on the floor in front of them all,
here in this elegant retirement center dining room.
Her arms had pulled in, and she'd leaned slightly forward—
almost like a contracted torso,
which had flexed, then had *stayed* flexed,
never returning to relaxation—
not far from an upright fetal position!
Sure, the ambulance was on its way now,
but, so what?
As helpful as they always tried to be,
this time it'd just be theatrics,
for, *this* contracted profile would not be straightening out.
Funny, how time had wounded her this way.
So, this was her last posture?
Well…let the others stare.
This was just how you looked…
when you still sat in your chair,
alone at your small, corner table…
here in this beautiful, elegant dining room…
assuming your last posture…
having an aneurysm of the aorta.

The Way Lost

Up and down the elevator,
in vertical exploration,
she would step out, then step back in,
with a peek at each hall, trying to recall
just where she had misplaced her way.
She lived somewhere, but where?
She should have recognized the floor,
but some strange spell
had come along
to unweave familiarity,
all halls now fallen
into a look all the same.
Or had recognition been the magic—
a good spell once here, but now gone?
As the door again opened,
she stepped out, but stepped back in.
When had this spell arrived
to leave her so near, yet leave her to wonder:
exactly which one was the floor
that she could not find anymore?

Pouring Night

A face wishing to reflect light
tenuously entered the abeyance
of a retirement center's waiting lounge
beside the empty dining room;
but, so far below the fallen day,
she found not light, but shadow,
come her way
to paint time with antithesis.

Well, nights came stronger now—
thicker and more deeply black.
There seemed, to her senses, less and less of day,
as though, soon, the day would not return, at all,
and only night loom there, in fall.
It would be harder to digest the deeper dark,
with no light's mix, at all.

Adjusting to the blackened hours,
her searching vision at last discerned
a brightly lit *ON* signal from a coffeepot.
All muscles on a visage once lovely
released themselves into exhale:
"Thank *heaven!*"— she softly whispered
across the solitude,
toward the smallest light in the night.

Then, while her hand fell painted with lonely mercy,
her eyes at last flashed answer to the bitter black.
She would not give it up because time had grown so strong.
No matter how stale the hours might taste,
or how unreflective their sight,
she would not put down the empty cup,
but still would pour the night…
and, although near the dregs at the bottom of time,
she would drink of time tonight, while she might.

Epilogue Clouds

Even the way bears tenure,
as a path, at last, regrows into the grass.
Down hints of the hall, now,
it looked like it might rain,
especially toward the very end,
where into its own epilogue
the hallway seemed to blend.
Yes, bright had it seemed
when he had left the apartment,
but you never could tell about inside weather.
The clear air could slip away.
Maybe he should have brought his old raincoat
to walk through a hall that had seemed to call his name.
Deep, dark clouds seemed forming, and it no longer looked the same
as when he'd begun, now that the light was slipping away,
for, under this ceiling of inside weather,
hadn't it turned into a foggy day?
Squinting down a life span of hall
toward where his thought must have gone—
through time that grew thicker as it grew deep—
his face seemed to blend with that thickening fog.
"It's growing so dark," he worried aloud…
then stepped toward an epilogue of clouds.

Discountenance

The rhythm doesn't fit:
Joe's trousers snapping past that fast.
They always followed his walker,
the only one with a bicycle horn,
timed to the rhythm that it takes to smile
when others react to the toot.
And, his sleeve that always leaves the handle
long enough to wave hello—
crossing this lobby, outward bound—
now seems too quickly to go.

But, both trousers and sleeve flop through the egress,
and both do take their leave,
for the clothes are full of emptiness—
exiting, hooked to a rack.
The hurried rack has lost Joe's gait,
and asks for no smile above it to wait.
Too cold, it rushes out the door.
Those clothes will never get their rhythm back,
and the walker horn will honk no more.
Joe is neither in those clothes
nor in the apartment anymore,
while removal of his name, there,
discountenances even a simple door.

The Dark at the Door

The dark has metaphorically knocked
at the healthcare door,
haunting my two-way radio:
"Funeral services wants in!"
Outside, reality has eerily curved into "wait"
while the departure vehicle idles, all in black—
as though arrived from death, itself…
and eager to return.

I wish the vehicle were not all black;
and, I wish the person were not
irretrievably still upstairs,
on the third floor,
lying just beyond the tenure of his life.
But I am the security guard.
I must force myself to acknowledge
the knock of death at the door,
then impel myself away from the light,
through this sense of death, toward it,
for, by fate and imperative,
it is I
who must unlock the door
to let in the ending.

The Walking Stick

No fingers curled into cheerful grasp
around the walking stick this morning
for it to tap into the early smells
and explore the rise of day.
It did not sense a smile form above it,
to hover there, and go with it,
no matter the turning of the way.
It did not descend the hill
to monitor the color of the tree leaves
or search for puddles to evince
rain's quiet fall from sleep.
Today, the walking stick
did not reprise the rhythm
of its rise and fall;
today, the walking stick
did not move at all.

It does not look right,
there where it tilts, alone,
in the corner near the door—
the door of an apartment
which soon will be rented to another.
It doesn't look the way it used to.
It should be out for a walk.
It looks like a mistake.
It looks too unwandered.
It looks too out of rhythm.
It looks too unleaned upon.
It looks…
too lonely.

The Return Trip

In a way, I am carrying air through the corridors,
a security guard who has been requested
to escort nothingness and emptiness from the healthcare side,
back to an apartment on the independent end.
I remember these cloth frames
when they were hosts to movement
that still wished and tried and even, at times, fell down.
I recall the many times I rushed to where they were
in order to pick them up, off the ground.
I remember how wrong it felt that they fell more and more,
while the wishing stayed strong inside.
It seemed so wrong that they could not stay high,
and have the spirit keep these clothes off the ground.
But, the strangest comprehension, just days ago,
was seeing they could no longer even posture upright
in a wheelchair to be pushed to the healthcare side,
but on a gurney were compelled to repose.
Toward that healthcare side I saw them go,
carrying their spirit within to that far, other side.
Now, in the aftermath,
it is I who must travel back to the start,
a surrogate on the long, return trip.
From the complex's very ending end,
back to the once living start,
I keep walking, with these in my arms.
I must carry the nothingness back through the halls,
really escorting nothing at all.
But, while memories dance toward the empty apartment,
as gently as I humanly can,
I do escort the air…
to take his empty clothes back there.

The Glass Dwelling

Aesthetically eloquent,
it casts sparkles up the carpeted avenues
from the plush entrance
if the sun hits it just right—
this glass dwelling,
this first residence beyond the double doors.
Such abode seems a
reward of resplendence,
commensurate with the efforts of a life
traveled all the way down time's road—
until now,
until time to live in the glass dwelling.

This shy resident
never asked to be transformed into bright symbol
and the centerpiece of cognizance be,
inside fine walls of ornate carvings,
for everyone who should pass to see.
But it is time, once more, for a metaphor.
It is time to exit plastered walls,
and in a vase repose;
for, here, on a table by the entrance,
near a sign that reads
"The retirement center is sad to announce…"
everyone turns into a rose.

Where Once Was Day

As I patrol where once was day,
I pray the night be still and undisturbed.
I pray into shadows
that they not descend into profundity
too deep for return to light.
I pray into the lurking ahead,
where I cannot see,
that there be nothing which waits for me.
I pray that the unhappened
may dismiss its urge to form,
and deem abeyance satisfactory
in this shapelessness
which precedes the new born day.

I bless each breeze while blowing
kindness across the fears,
and thank the air for alarm-free silence
while the breezes wait.
I thank all past adversity
for turning to courage inside me
from lessons of life's road.
And I praise the stars for subtle shine
as I patrol time's long decline.

I pray the night be still and undisturbed;
and, if it agrees, I, too, will remain like that,
undisturbed through the fall of hours,
accompanying them in their deepening way,
if only I may know the dawn will really come
to render exorable
this lonely residence
in the black below the day.

Twilight of Dreams

I walk the after path
of the denizens of dreams.
Their wishing now has largely
fallen into shadow,
for day has almost used its stay,
while light toward night must slowly bend.
Shadows form where the hours were
—where resplendence glared, thick,
and where it glared, thin—
and it is time for my patrol again,
for each evening, at ten,
time sends me down these retirement center byways,
past room after room of those I know,
who are slipping from the light.
I find myself compelled to join the dimness
as my security guard hand must reach for switches
to extinguish half the illumination;
yet, as I watch every other glow go out,
so, too, do I see every second glow live on.
And, slowly, in weak beauty,
I sense that
it is twilight which forms
through these halls of last dreams.

About the Author

Born in 1945, Tom met his wife Loretta at Penn State. They have three daughters and three grandsons. Tom's poetry and/or fiction has appeared in eleven countries in such publications as *Poetry Ireland* (Dublin), *Poetry Canada*, *Voices Israel*, *Storie* (Rome), *The Plaza* (Tokyo), *Seattle Review*, *Portland Review*, *Poetry New York*, *Journal of the American Medical Association* and *South Carolina Review*. After retiring from the U.S. Postal Service, Tom became a security guard at a retirement/healthcare facility. The drama of dream and vulnerability found there has transmuted into *Twilight of Dreams*.

www.ingramcontent.com/pod-product-compliance
Lightning Source LLC
Chambersburg PA
CBHW071026080526
44587CB00015B/2516